Up from the Ground

Connecting Kids to Real Food

A garden-based workbook for kids

by Rebecca Murakami

This book belongs to:

ISBN-13: 978-1-7343995-0-9

"If I were growing in the garden, I would be a *marigold* so I don't get eaten by bugs!"
- Helen, age 10

"If I were growing in the garden, I would be a *raspberry* – because it's so sweet and flavor-y."
- Madelyn, age 8

"If I were growing in the garden I'd be a *cherry* to watch the birds."
- Anna, age 11

"If I were growing in the garden I'd be a *carrot* because they're tall and skinny."
- Calvin, age 8

Welcome to <u>Up From the Ground!</u>

After 10 years of enjoying the benefits of gardening with my own kids, I knew it was time to help other kids connect with Real Food too. Spring peas, rich kale, sweet cherry tomatoes, juicy raspberries and edible flowers have all made their way into playtime and mealtime at our house. What my kids didn't suspect until I intentionally taught them about it, is that they also benefit from connecting with the soil that their food grows in. Knowing that beneficial soil bacteria contributes to good health (especially a strong digestive tract and immune system) I've never been too much of a stickler about washing our own garden vegetables before eating. We even have a compost play station in the backyard. I want my children to reap the benefits of not only the ripe perfection of homegrown food, but also of the homegrown microorganisms in the soil and on the food we harvest from the garden.

Research says that connecting with soil, and most importantly, the beneficial microorganisms in the soil contributes to our health, well-being and even the very basis of who we are. I hope that this workbook will inspire curiosity and a sense of empowerment while the concerns about "bugs" and "dirt" fade away.

Truly, more than plants grow up from the ground. Kids do too. Kids grow strong bodies and minds from a whole-foods based diet, but even more importantly, they grow from a real connection to the soil – the place where life begins. The miracle of soil is that it recycles nutrients, integrates water, supports microbial life and even captures the sun's energy to nourish the entire planet. It all begins and ends with the soil.

This workbook explores that grand cycle we call "seasons" and the role of soil and edible plants in it.

This workbook is most useful if there is a garden, or a garden box, available to your kids or students. As you use this workbook, encourage kids to engage their senses. Observe colors, touch the soil, and breathe deeply. This will make a lasting impression, connecting them with our rich earth, the origin of food and set them up to appreciate the value of whole food. It need not be complicated. The simplicity of soil, a seed, sun and water is a lesson that will nourish them throughout life.

As you get started, connect with the head gardener at the garden you will visit and make arrangements for activities ahead of time. Ask what they will be planting and how you can best participate. It can be a challenge to keep little toes from stepping on plants and little fingers from pulling the wrong things. Talk together about how to help kids be successful in the garden. Become familiar with where things like rakes and buckets are kept and help your students to clean up after themselves. Wash hands with a mild, fragrance free soap, like Dr. Bronner's castile soap, when returning to class.

My vision is to restore the position of the edible garden to the place where nourishment is found. And thus to nourish our kids. Grocery store vegetables are not the perfect replacement for homegrown vegetables. We gain so much more when we step into the garden to discover, contribute and create. This kind of nourishment will do much to strengthen kids in the face of modern stressors. Teaching kids that they grow "up from the ground" is the cornerstone to a healthy life and a loved planet.

To nourishing our kids,

 Rebecca

I like eating from the garden and the feel of the soil. Garden food tastes fresh. The soil is soft. It makes me feel alive! Picking and eating fresh berries from the garden is the best! Berries from the store taste sour, but berries from our garden taste just right. I love growing things to share with others, especially zucchini! I can't imagine our yard without a garden. Kids should play in the garden because it's energizing!
I've loved to pick and eat chives with my friend next door since we were little. Now we pick and eat calendula and pansies too!
- Helen, age 10

I like to help mulch the cucumber patch. My favorite things to eat in the garden are potatoes, blueberries and lettuce. Roly polies are tickly and fun! I'm thankful that our garden is so, so very pretty. – Madelyn, age 8

One favorite memory is picking carrots with my grandma. They cover the driveway, there are so many! – Anna, age 11

I love pulling weeds with my grandma. It's satisfying...there are thousands of them! – Calvin, age 8

How to use this workbook

This book is best used wherever children and space for a garden come together. It's intended for ages 3-10. Modifications can easily be made to suit the age that you are working with. The workbook pages, with 5 pages for each season, guide the experience for each child. This will be their place to express the observations and connections they've made in the garden that day.

If there are months of the year that your class or group of children do not meet, that's okay. Just pick up with the teaching whenever you can. Many school schedules don't include July or August, but there is still plenty of summer to be found in June and September.

For each season, refer to the corresponding Teacher's Page at the beginning of the book. Each season focuses on a topic inspired by what is happening in the garden. Here you will find *teaching prompts, suggested activities and ideas for the workbook pages*. There are also suggested books, Take a Look Books, to read with students that supports the topic for that season. Of course, there are many others available. These particular Take a Look Books have been chosen because they highlight the intended learning for that season.

I suggest pre-teaching from the teaching prompts and a Take a Look Book before visiting the garden.

Choose one or more activities and coordinate with the head gardener in advance of your visit. (Don't have an established garden or gardener to coordinate with? See Appendix E for ideas.) Bring the workbooks (and crayons or colored pencils) when the students visit the garden. It doesn't matter if they get a little dirty. Just keep them in a dry place until after the activity is finished, then allow students to complete a workbook page with the prompts from the Teacher's Page or their own self-directed learning. There are 5 pages for each season so that students can interact with the garden several times in a season. This will allow them to see growth and other changes over time.

The garden experience provides inspiration for further learning as you return to the classroom. Art projects, math story problems, writing – let your students continue to create and learn!

My intention is that together with the teaching, the workbook creates an opportunity for kids to not only get dirty in the garden, but to engage with it through the seasons. The soil is the basis for all of this. So getting (at least a little) dirty is an important part of the learning and growth that happens here!

Remind kids not to taste until they ask. See appendices for *class-friendly recipes, further resources and Washington Administrative Code (WAC)-friendly garden suggestions*.

 **Late Winter: Soil**

Take a look books

> It's a Good Thing There are Earthworms by Jodie Shepherd (younger ages)
> Earthworms by Elaine Pascoe (older ages)

Teaching prompts

- Our food needs sunlight, water and soil to grow.
- Soil provides nutrients, structure and good bacteria needed to grow healthy plants for eating.
- We can help create healthy soil by covering it with mulch and adding compost underneath the mulch. Growing food removes nutrients from the soil. Adding more to the soil than we take away ensures a good harvest every year.
- Creatures like earthworms living in the soil also help make healthy soil. We can give them a safe place to live and grow so they can help us grow better food.

Activities

1. Look at the soil covering (mulch) or top layer of soil. What is it made of? What does it look like underneath? Underneath it is breaking down or decaying. How does mulch help grow yummy plants to eat? It protects soil from washing away in the rain, warms soil in the spring, helps rainwater get into soil, and makes compost/decayed matter. Organic matter from compost provides good nutrition (like vitamins) and lots of good or beneficial bacteria. It's a good place for many creatures to live. We need little creatures in the soil to grow the best food!
2. With fingers, small rakes or forks, gently dig through top layer of soil. Look under rocks, too. Pull out worms. Let kids hold them. Teach them to be gentle with them. What other creatures do they find? Make observations.
3. Observe the weather. How does that affect the soil?

Workbook (Bring workbook to the garden)

- Draw worms and other creatures found. Measure them.
- What colors are in the garden now?
- What's the weather like today? How does that change the soil?
- What do you see in the soil?
- What plants are growing now?

Spring: Planting

Take a look books
> Up in the Garden and Down in the Dirt by Kate Messner (younger kids)
> Anywhere Farm by Phyllis Root (all ages)
> We are the Gardeners by Joanna Gaines (older kids)

Teaching prompts
- Spring is the time when we plant most vegetables. Some plants like the cooler weather of early spring, others like to be planted when it's warmer. We can plant seeds that will grow into plants or we can plant small plants called "seedlings" to help give them a head start. (When they are bigger, things like slugs and rabbits are less likely to eat them all.)
- Sometimes plants, like strawberries, are already growing in the ground. The green plant the berries grow from can live in the soil through the winter. We will see white flowers. Berries will grow from these flowers. The berries are green at first. We eat them when they are ripe or when they are red.
- Herbs, like Rosemary, Thyme and Sage can also grow through the winter. These herbs smell really good and flavor other foods when we cook.
- Peas and lettuce are two types of vegetables that like to grow in the cooler spring weather.

Activity
1. Strawberries look for white flowers/green berries (don't touch yet!) and ripe berries.
2. Identify rosemary, thyme and sage. Run hands gently along the stems of rosemary and thyme and gently rub sage leaves (no need to cut or pluck leaves). Smell fingers.
3. Plant snow pea and lettuce seedlings in rows as directed by garden manager.
4. Weekly or twice a week, check on plants – how are the strawberry flowers changing? Are your pea plants and lettuce still green? How have they changed?
5. Show kids which plants are weeds. Have them pull a few weeds to make room for strawberries/peas/lettuce to grow. (Weeding is an important activity in the garden. Learning early to do it normalizes it and reinforces the idea that we can help our plants be healthy and strong.)
6. Breathe deeply. What does spring smell like? What does the soil smell like?
7. Create a strawberry, pea and lettuce salad for snack. (See Appendix A)

Workbook (Bring workbook to the garden)
- Strawberries/Peas/Pea Tendrils/Lettuce: observe, draw, measure, touch, taste, smell, create
    - Which plants are growing? How are the seedlings changing?
- What colors do you see in the garden?
- How does the soil feel?
- Draw the herbs you find.

 Summer: Water and Beneficial Insects

Take a look books

> It's a Good Thing there are Ladybugs by Joanne Mattern (younger kids)
> You Wouldn't Want to Live without Insects by Anne Rooney (older kids)

Teaching Prompts

- Summer weather is hot. Plants need water to grow. Sometimes water comes from rain but there isn't always enough rain. That means that plants will need extra water to grow strong and produce vegetables and fruit. The gardener needs to make sure the plants always get enough water. What are some ways the gardener can water their plants? (sprinkler, drip irrigation, watering can)
- Which vegetables grow best in hot summer weather? (zucchini, cucumber, green beans, tomatoes)
- What do you think of insects? Do you think insects can be helpful in the garden? One insect that hurts plants in the garden is called an aphid. They suck plant juices out of the leaves, stems and roots of plants. This harms the plants and makes it difficult for them to grow. Aphids are a common garden problem in the summer. Aphids eat plants, but guess who eats aphids? Ladybugs! We can help our garden grow nutritious food by adding ladybugs to the garden.
- What are some other beneficial insects? (spiders, praying mantis, green lacewings)

Activity

1. Talk to the head gardener about how they make sure the garden always has enough water. (How? How often? How much?)
2. Water plants with a watering can.
3. Find and harvest zucchini, cucumber, green beans and tomatoes (Math: count or make story problems from harvested vegetables.)
4. Look for aphids. How big are they? Are they alone? What plants do they like? Look under leaves. Count aphids.
5. Release ladybugs (purchase from local garden store).
8. Find herbs: parsley, basil, and cilantro. Run hands gently along the stems and leaves (no need to cut or pluck leaves). Smell fingers.
6. Breathe deeply. What does summer smell like?
7. Create Cucumber Tomato Basil salad in the garden (See Appendix A).
8. Create Zucchini Ribbon Salad (See Appendix A).
9. Create Seasonal Fruit Salad (See Appendix A).

Workbook (Bring workbook to the garden)

- Measure and draw aphid, ladybug.
- Measure and draw additional insects found.
- Zucchini, cucumber, green beans, and tomatoes: observe, draw, measure, touch, taste.

Fall: Garden Clean Up and Winter Preparation

Take a look books

> Discover Dirt by Pamela Hall (younger kids)
>
> Jump into Science: Dirt by Steve Tomecek (older kids)

Teaching Prompts

- Growing food follows the seasons of the year. Like summer, fall is a season of harvest. Many squash and tree fruits are ready for eating.
- When plants are finished producing food or a frost freezes the plants, we can cut and remove the plants. We can put them in the compost pile to decompose and recycle their nutrients.
- Fall is also the time that we prepare the garden for the winter. The garden soil needs to rest and be recharged for the spring. What we do in the fall gets the soil ready for planting next spring. This completes the cycle of seasons and of life in the garden.
- Getting ready for winter means covering the soil. Placing a layer of mulch over the soil provides rest, protection and nourishment. Covering soil protects it from washing away in the rain, warms soil in the spring, helps rainwater get into soil, and makes compost/decayed matter. Adding compost under the mulch adds valuable insects, microbes and nutrients. Compost feeds soil. Soil feeds plants. The garden uses the resting time provided by winter to grow strong plants and nutritious food next spring and summer.

Activity

1. Observe and harvest winter squash, beets, apples, plums, etc.
2. Remove plants after a frost. Choose plants that will pull out easily, like summer squash.
3. Take turns spreading mulch with a rake. Apply thin layer of compost underneath if possible.
4. Breathe deeply. What does fall smell like?
5. Create Zucchini Ribbon Salad (See Appendix A).
6. Create Seasonal Fruit Salad (See Appendix A).
7. Create Roasted Pumpkin Seeds (See Appendix A).

Workbook (Bring workbook to the garden)

- What does the garden look like now? Draw a picture.
- What vegetables are ready to harvest?
- What colors do you see?
- What plants are still growing? What plants can be removed?

Name:

What does your garden look like? Draw it.

Date:

Today's observations:

What creatures do you find in the soil?

Observe. Measure. Draw. Touch. Taste. Smell.

1

2

3

4

5

6

7

Date:

Today's observations:

What colors are in the garden now?

Observe. Measure. Draw. Touch. Taste. Smell.

Date:

Today's observations:

1

2

3

4

5

6

What's the weather like today?

Observe. Measure. Draw. Touch. Taste. Smell.

7

Date:

Today's observations:

What do you see in the soil?

Observe. Measure. Draw. Touch. Taste. Smell.

Date:

Today's observations:

What is growing in the garden today?

Observe. Measure. Draw. Touch. Taste. Smell.

1

2

3

4

5

6

7

Date:

Today's observations:

What does spring smell like?

Observe. Measure. Draw. Touch. Taste. Smell.

Date:

Today's observations:

What colors do you see in the garden?

1

2

3

4

5

6

7

Observe. Measure. Draw. Touch. Taste. Smell.

Date:

Today's observations:

What plants are beginning to come up?

Observe. Measure. Draw. Touch. Taste. Smell.

Date:

Today's observations:

How does the soil feel?

Observe. Measure. Draw. Touch. Taste. Smell.

1

2

3

4

5

6

7

Date:

Today's observations:

Which herbs can you find?

Observe. Measure. Draw. Touch. Taste. Smell.

Place or draw seeds in the spaces below. Find additional seeds for the remaining spaces.

Apple	Cucumber	Carrot	Pea
Pumpkin	Green Bean	Garlic	Zucchini
Kale	Lettuce	Cilantro	Beet
Tomato	Plum		

Date:

Today's observations:

What insects do you see?

Observe. Measure. Draw. Touch. Taste. Smell.

Date:

Today's observations:

What colors are in the garden today?

Observe. Measure. Draw. Touch. Taste. Smell.

1

2

3

4

5

6

7

Date:

Today's observations:

What does the soil feel like? What do you think it needs?

Observe. Measure. Draw. Touch. Taste. Smell.

Date:

Today's observations:

What do the flowers smell like?

Observe. Measure. Draw. Touch. Taste. Smell.

1
2
3
4
5
6
7

Date:

Today's observations:

How many aphids do you see?
Can the ladybugs eat them all?

Observe. Measure. Draw. Touch. Taste. Smell.

Date:

Today's observations:

What plants are ready to harvest?

Observe. Measure. Draw. Touch. Taste. Smell.

1

2

3

4

5

6

7

Date:

Today's observations:

What colors do you see?

Observe. Measure. Draw. Touch. Taste. Smell.

Date:

Today's observations:

What plants are still growing?

Observe. Measure. Draw. Touch. Taste. Smell.

1

2

3

4

5

6

7

Date:

Today's observations:

What plants can be cut or removed?

Observe. Measure. Draw. Touch. Taste. Smell.

Date:

Today's observations:

What does fall smell like?

Observe. Measure. Draw. Touch. Taste. Smell.

1
2
3
4
5
6
7

If you were growing in the garden, what would you be? Why?

Draw it here.

Name, age _____

Garden Seasons & Activities

Soil is alive! Taking care of it grows the best harvest. Yum!

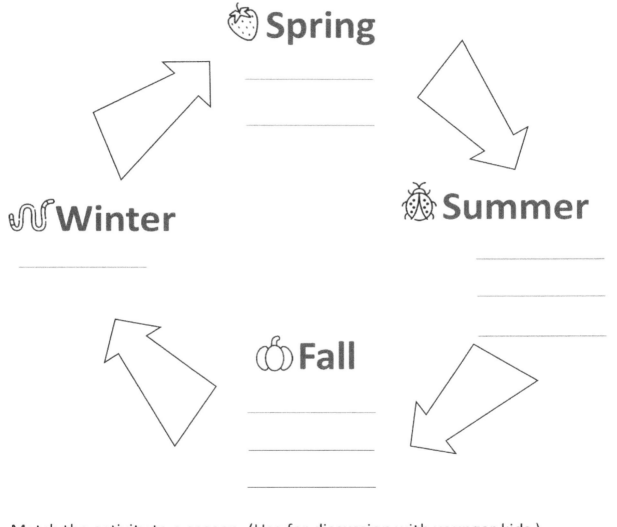

🍓 **Spring**

_____

_____

🐞 **Summer**

_____

_____

🎃 **Fall**

_____

_____

_____

🪱 **Winter**

_____

Match the activity to a season. (Use for discussion with younger kids.)

Rest soil	Clean up old plants	Plant
Weed	Prepare soil	Add Ladybugs
Harvest	Water	

Garden Seasons & Activities Key

Winter – rest soil
Spring – plant, weed
Summer – water, add ladybugs
Fall – clean up old plants, prepare soil, harvest
>>>Some activities can be done in more than one season.

Glossary

(Late Winter)
Beneficial Bacteria – Types of bacteria that benefit human, animal and plant health. Most bacteria help, not harm, people and plants.
Compost – Decayed plants used as a fertilizer.
Nutrition – Vitamins, minerals and other substances in plants necessary for growing a healthy life.
Organic Matter – Part of soil, broken down (decayed) plants and animals that adds nutrients and structure to the soil that plants need to grow.

(Spring)
Herbs – Usually thought of as the plants in the garden used to flavor other foods. Have a strong scent and flavor. Can also be medicinal.
Seeds – Nature's tiny packages that we plant in the ground to grow more plants.
Seedlings – Small plants grown in greenhouses that can be planted directly into the garden instead of seeds.

(Summer)
Aphids – Small insects that can destroy plants by sucking out the plant juices.
Beneficial Insects – Insects that promote health of the garden and plants.
Ladybugs – Beneficial insects that eat aphids (up to 5,000 in its lifetime!). Part of the beetle family.

(Fall)
Harvest – Picking fruits, vegetables and other edible plants that are ready to be eaten.
Mulch – Protective covering of small plant pieces (like chipped wood, leaves) spread over the ground to improve soil and plant life.

Appendix A: Garden fresh recipes

These are truly garden fresh recipes simply designed so that you and your students are the creators. No cooking is necessary for most of them, just some simple prep work that can be done on the spot in the garden or in the classroom. I suggest gathering the supplies in a basket to bring to the garden. It's delightful to enjoy what you create in the place where it was grown!

<u>Strawberry, Pea (pea pods or tendrils) and Lettuce Salad</u> (Spring)
- Supplies: cutting board, small knife, lettuce spinner (if desired), bowl, serving spoon, small paper cups, toothpicks, olive oil.
- Teacher: Cut strawberries and pea pods or tendrils into bite size pieces. Toss with olive oil.
- Students: Tear the lettuce and mix in bowl with strawberries and pea pods/tendrils.

<u>Tomato Cucumber Basil Salad</u> (Summer)
- Supplies: cutting board, small knife, Himalayan salt, olive oil, bowl, serving spoon, toothpicks, small paper cups.
- Teacher: Slice vegetables, drizzle with salt and olive oil.
- Students: Tear the basil and toss the salad.

<u>Zucchini Ribbon Salad</u> (Summer/Fall)
- Supplies: Vegetable peeler (more than one if you want kids to participate), small knife, cutting board, bowl, serving spoon, small paper cups, toothpicks, lemon, Himalayan salt, pepper, garlic, olive oil.
- Teacher: chop garlic, supervise using peeler to create ribbons from zucchini. Use green or yellow zucchini and any other brightly vegetable that you can create a ribbon from (i.e. carrots) by running the peeler lengthwise over it. Drizzle olive oil.
- Students: Ribbon the zucchini or other vegetables used, squeeze lemon, add salt and pepper. Toss the salad.

<u>Seasonal Fruit Salad</u> (Summer/Fall)
- Supplies: 2 or more ripe fruits from the garden. Herbs like basil or mint. Small knife, cutting board, bowl, serving spoon, small paper cups, toothpicks.
- Teacher: Cut fruits as needed.
- Students: Tear herbs and toss with fruits.

<u>Roasted Pumpkin Seeds</u> (Great opportunity for students to enjoy a fall classic! Oven required.)
- Supplies: Knife, spoon, bowl, salt (about 1 TBLS), pumpkin.
- Teacher: Open pumpkin, allow seeds to soak overnight, roast in oven with additional salt.
- Students: Lift out pumpkin seeds, place in bowl with salt and cover with water.

Appendix B: Extra fun garden tips. Try it!

- Grow and harvest potatoes
- Grow edible flowers – make a flower salad
- Measure how much a zucchini grows in a day or in a week in August
- Enjoy a roly poly (potato bug) play date
- Taste the rainbow - Find edibles in the colors of the rainbow
- Grow gigantic sunflowers – watch their heads follow the sun, harvest seeds
- Collect seeds of weeds, flowers, edibles – draw, compare, make art, etc.

Appendix C: Additional resources for adults

- Access the Up from the Ground educational YouTube playlist. www.upfromthegroundbook.com
- The Dirt Cure, Growing Healthy Kids with Food Straight from Soil, by Maya Shetreat-Klein, MD.
- 100 Days of Real Food on a Budget, by Lisa Leake. Blog and Book.
- www.RodaleInstitute.org Growing the organic movement through research, farmer training, and consumer education.
- Rodale Organic Gardening Basics – soil, by Rodale, Inc.
- Learn more about Regenerative Agriculture. www.kisstheground.com/videos
- Beecher's Foundation, youth programs - Sparking curiosity about what's really in the foods kids eat, raising awareness about how food companies are marketing to kids, teaching kids how to read nutrition labels and ingredient lists.

Appendix D: Additional Washington Administrative Code (WAC) friendly garden suggestions

- Gardens should be located away from sources of contamination
- Use barriers, like fencing, netting or cages to keep pets away from garden
- Use water from a public water system or a private well
- Materials for borders, raised beds or trellises must not leach chemicals into soil
- Do not use chemical pesticides
- Actively supervise children where commonplace toxic plants/leaves are growing (ie rhubarb)

Appendix E: Tips for when there is no established garden

- Locate a space where a garden bed or planter box can be created. Choose a space with access to water that has a minimum of 6 hours of direct sun. Protect with a short fence or netting.
- Consider beginning in the fall so the soil has time to mature over winter. Add compost and cover with mulch.
- Consider making a worm bin.
- Consult a planting calendar for your area like this one: www.almanac.com/gardening/planting-calendar
- Plant seedlings instead of seeds.
- Don't strive for perfection. Success can be as simple as getting little hands in the soil and growing just a few productive plants.
- Use the "Take a Look Books" listed in the teacher's pages and the Up from the Ground garden education YouTube playlist to start learning. Access the playlist here: www.upfromthegroundbook.com

Access the Up from the Ground
educational YouTube playlist and more at:

www.upfromthegroundbook.com

Acknowledgements

Thank you to my children's grandparents – lovingly caring for my youngest while I create. Thank you to Rod, Nancy and Gail, well-qualified educators who enthusiastically reviewed and contributed to my work. Thank you to John Martinson, the garden manager for the Real Life Church garden, providing food for the Storehouse foodbank and the opportunity for kids to connect with soil. Mr. Martinson believes in the value of organically grown food for everyone, sharing his life to make it a reality. Harvesting potatoes in his garden with my kids was a real joy!

Garden icons made by Freepik from www.flaticon.com
Cover illustration and design by Ira Baykovska
Author photo by Andrea Renee Photography

Your purchase of this book is appreciated! Please take a moment to review <u>Up from the Ground</u> on Amazon. This is the best way for independent authors to gain exposure and help sales. Thank you!

Made in the USA
Coppell, TX
19 January 2020